We Three Queens

by

Valerie Simmons-Langhorn

For Bookings email: unlimitfavor@aol.com

Artwork Created by: Felicia Matthews, Austin, TX
Pre Editor: Rhonda Ross
Final Editing: Valinda Wynn
Manuscript Prepared by: Native Productions,
Hampton, VA
ISBN: 978-0615999944

DEDICATION

First, I dedicate this book to three queens who have left an indelible impression on my life. In countless ways, I credit these women, whether by design or Providence, with molding me into the person I am today.

Foremost is my mother, Lucinda, whom I affectionately call "Mommy". The quintessential mother of seven children; a lover of all people, kind-hearted, and affectionate. Mommy, the ideal nurturer, instructed my siblings and I to demonstrate charity amongst ourselves, not to allow envy or contention to take root within us, and to unconditionally accept our individual and collective faults. In fact, Mommy staunched any rivalries and counterproductive squabbles we could have initiated with each other. That kind of thing was just not tolerated, under any circumstances.

I acknowledge Mommy with being the catalyst used by God to instill my initial hunger and thirst for righteousness. Because of her Christ centered life and godly example, I knew I would also embrace Jesus, someday. As a matter of fact, I learned how to be a *"virtuous woman"* to my husband as I watched Mommy then and continue to gain insight from her daily. Words cannot adequately express how significant my Mommy is to me. I love her dearly and I, along with my siblings, believe she is the greatest mother in the world.

I salute my mom and all the mothers of the world for being the best. Thank you, Mommy, for caring and loving, providing and never denying. You are better than best, to me.

The second queen is Lady Vivian F. Green, the late wife of my pastor, Bishop Samuel L. Green, Jr. Lady Green was an excellent model of how to be a *"good thing"* to your husband. Her methods, in many ways, mirrored those of my mother. She was soft-spoken, compassionate, and kind. I regret her passing before the completion of my first writing. However, in gratitude, I say, thank you, Lady Green for your life, your example, and your legacy. You are sorely missed and will be remembered, forever.

Lastly, the third queen is Evangelist Maria Gardner of Philadelphia, Pennsylvania, who in 1974, as a young and anointed vessel of God, took the time to introduce her audience to the love of Christ (known as "the altar call"), at a church that would become my spiritual refuge for over thirty years. It was after experiencing Evangelist Gardner's anointed ministry, I decided to make Jesus my choice. I do not remember what she said to trigger the call in my life, but I will forever be grateful for her obedience to God. Thank you, Evangelist/Pastor Maria Gardner, for your passion for Christ.

I love these three queens for the huge impression and influence they have had on and in my life. I thank God for them.

There are many other queens who have impacted my life - too many to list. I will mention a few more, though, namely, my three sisters, Marjorie, Lucy, and Gwen. I enjoy the time we share with each other. Eagerly I anticipate and enjoy the time we share together; it is not nearly as often as any of us would like. Immeasurable is my love for all of them.

The last three queens are mentioned because their impressions in my life are so varied and unique. The queen who invited me to church on a Friday night I will never forget, Janice (JJ). She has been a dear friend ever since that night. Where would I be today, if you had not taken the time to WITNESS and invite me to the place to meet THE KING of all kings? Wow! Thanks, Janice.

Next, is Margie Mary, the money magnet. Maybe, if I stick close enough to you, some of that financial acumen will rub off on me. I love you, more than you understand.

The last queen has been my friend, pal, buddy, and sister for over 35 years.

Nothing more needs to be said. Nell, thanks for the company.

THE QUEENS COME IN THREE'S. AMAZING!

I cannot end this dedication and not share with you the three kings of my life. The first king is the late Mr. Charlie Simmons, affectionately, known as Mr. C., my dad. This man instilled in me, and my siblings, the importance of hard work and honesty. My dad passed at the young age of 89 and remained the tower of strength for our family. I love you, Dad.

My pastor, Bishop Green, is one of the greatest teachers and mentors anyone could have. He taught me how to live holy, maintain my integrity, walk humbly before God, live positively, and enjoy life. Most importantly, he taught and showed me laughter really is like medicine; it is indeed a healer. I never forget my daily dose of laughter. Thank you, Bishop.

Last, but, most certainly, not least, is Calvin, my husband. Calvin is my love, friend, and constant inspiration; I thank him for allowing me the space and time to complete this book. Initially, neither of us knew the direction my writing would take. Yet, he never discouraged or dissuaded me from it. After over thirty years of being a couple, I love him more today than the day of our marriage. Love you, CB.

By the way, my four brothers and kings, Chuck, David, Daniel, and Ray are marvelous, also.

CONTENTS

1 A QUEEN

QUEEN A, hails from a large family of seven sisters and six brothers. From the outside looking in, her father treated her mother like a queen. He waited on her (as the old folks would say), *"hand and foot."* He took good care of the family and they did extremely well.

Even though she witnessed the love and care between her parents, Queen A did not expect or embrace those traits in her own relationship. Therefore, after many years of marriage, she left her husband. Only returning, later, when he became ill, to nurse him until his death. Now Queen A lives to take care of another man - a married one.

~QUEEN A~

She worked hard and commanded a respectable salary. A lot of her money was spent on her lover. Although this man had a wife and family, she escorted him to parties and other gatherings, as if they were married.

They lived in different states, believing the possibility of him being seen consorting with another woman, outside of his marriage, was improbable. Neither of them had concern about their indiscretions or ramifications if they had been discovered. Their affair had been in effect for many years.

She spoke of her lover as a wife would

about her husband. Yet she was far from being that. Queen A did not realize no amount of complaining about her lover's wife or his promises to legitimize their affair would have made him leave his marriage. Her chiding with him was useless. He would not change for her or anyone. Her comments were like a *"cry in the wilderness"* – wasted breath.

Some say no commitment exists in an adulterous relationship. Yet, Queen A was committed to giving her married lover what he wanted physically and sexually, and was available whenever he requested her time. Unfortunately, she would also, unknowingly, reap the consequences of her actions because the Bible says, *"Be not deceived; God is not mocked; for whatsoever a man or woman soweth, that shall he or she also reap."* **Galatians 6:7**

If Queen A ever decided to remarry, she should remember, somewhere, a woman would be ready to become her husband's mistress, just as she was willing to be with her lover. Queen A said, *"No strings attached."* But strings were attached; they were invisible and intangible. In retrospect, she would never agree to share her husband with another woman.

The conclusion is this, a woman who becomes a mistress does not love herself and by choosing this lifestyle she hinders her future. Precious time and energy are wasted on a circumstance in which a mistress does not usually win. So listen up, Queen A; time to start loving yourself.

2

FOR LOVE OR MONEY

Many women, in and out of the church, find it sometimes difficult to marry for the right reasons. There are many reasons (especially in these difficult times) one would marry. Unfortunately, for some, those reasons could haunt them, later.

In a marriage where the woman marries for or because of love, that marriage could work for a while; but if that love is not cherished, nourished, and cultivated the least thing could cause love to diminish or grow cold. Money, or the lack thereof, can cause a rift in a marriage, if the couple or spouse mismanages the household funds.

Will love keep this relationship together? Maybe, maybe not. One thing for sure, a budget is necessary. It requires communication between the couple, to implement. The man has to give his wife hope that better days will come for them and enforce adherence to the household allowance or he will not be considered head of his home. Conversations between the couple should be positive and encouraging and the husband should contribute financially to the home.

Unfortunately, if there is continuous financial struggle and lack, even though the wife works to help make ends meet, in the long run, the marriage and love could suffer. Again, if love is not maintained and strengthened, as time goes on, it will fail the test of time, especially during the hard ones.

Now, take a look at the woman who married the love of her dreams. The marriage did not suffer because of the lack of money. The wife had everything she wanted and needed, except her husband's time and attention. The problem was she was lonely and unhappy. All of her husband's attention was on making more money, work, work, and more work, while she stayed home – bored and depressed. She had been encouraged to volunteer for a charity, to keep herself occupied. However, nothing replaced the attention and affection of her husband. This woman had everything when it pertained to things, but it was obvious, the things did not make her happy.

She honestly married because she

loved her husband and hoped her love would be reciprocated. He, on the other hand, believed the things she received from him should have kept her happy. There are women who desire to be loved. These women would rather have their husband's time and attention, than a mink coat. This queen was one of them. Yet, some still called her a fool. She believed *"love covers a multitude of sins"* from **I Peter 4:8b**. This wife should have been able to have the mink coat, affection, and attention of her husband.

Love does not hurt, but loneliness does. Living with a man who pays attention to everyone and everything else, hurts. The woman who is content with just things has a flaw in her character.

For centuries, women have been living under the assumption and notion that the wife should be satisfied under any circumstances, as long as the bills are paid and regardless of whether the husband comes home at night. Not so! He should accept his part in contributing to the loneliness his wife endures. She needs him for more than the mortgage payment and expensive jewelry.

His actions are comparable to those who use hush money to prevent public knowledge of a trespass. In this case, the husband gives his wife whatever she wants, keeps the bills paid, and maintains the household; however, his wife is never to mention where he fails concerning her. This man believes, as long as he gives his wife money and possessions, nothing should be said about his extra-marital activities.

Well, the pimp provides things for his *"ladies of the night"*, but that does not legitimize prostitution. Consequently, neither does a man supplying his wife with material comforts justify him neglecting her other needs.

Marriages and relationships based on care, respect, and concern for the other are probably the happiest. What is the most honorable estate? Is it marrying for love or marrying for money? The answer is subjective and either decision has its risks with no guarantee of a happy ending. However, getting married without good, godly counsel is not wise for couples to do. Remember, *"In a multitude of counsel, there is safety."* **Proverbs 11:14b**.

3
QUEEN B

QUEEN B married who she called *"a crazy dude."* To this union, a beautiful baby girl was born; unfortunately, her husband never learned his spousal role. He worked, periodically, but instead of having a house his wife could call home, he moved into the one she acquired prior to their marriage.

Things were off from the beginning. The *"crazy dude"* wanted marriage to get a VISA. The guilt trip Queen B suffered just contemplating his deportation was sufficient enough for her to oblige his unspoken proposal of marriage. This is her story.

~QUEEN B~

He agreed to go with her in the "love" business as long as she wanted, initially. He appeared to be just what she desired in a man. The kind who helped around the house, cooked, cleaned, manicured the lawn, and serviced her car.

After she dated him a while, he informed her they must marry, immediately. He convinced her not to wait, any longer. But what he omitted to disclose was his motivation for wanting to marry was not love for her but fear of missing his citizenship deadline. If he intended to stay in America, he could not tell her why they had to marry. He knew she would not agree. He shrewdly played the role of a great catch. Because of that, she decided not to wait any longer.

This man had ulterior motives and did not stop until he got what he wanted. He knew what, how, and when to say or do the right thing to accomplish his purpose. He was patient and made good use of his time while he waited. He worked on his victim's psyche to disarm her, make her question her self-worth, self-esteem, and seek validation from him, which he rationed out to her, sparingly – for control - manipulating her to his whims. He may have said, *"You have done well for yourself."* He may have asked, *"You really bought this house on your own?"* Or even commented, *"It is amazing how long you have been on that job."*

He was the type of man who made women believe they could not make it without him and made statements like,

"You need me," or *"We could do so much more if we were married,"* and *"If you were married to me, we could expand this business, remodel the house, and add to your bank account."*

One of her responses should have been, *"Where is your house or your business so we can remodel and expand them,"* and *"How much money do you have in your bank account?"* But, some women never attempt to analyze the disparity between what they and their partners have accomplished – and she was one of those women. This man had spun a web congested with manipulative psychological games that birthed in her feelings of incompetence, powerlessness, and uncertainty in her abilities to thrive without his presence, input, or approval.

Against her better judgment, Queen B married this man. Soon after, she became a victim of his emotional and verbally abusive behavior. According to him, she no longer did any thing correctly. Neither was she worthy, in his eyes, to be his wife. Yet, in the midst of all the negativity and turmoil, an innocent child was born.

After a while, this queen forgot who she was. She unwittingly sold control of her life to her mate. She was not allowed to think independent of her husband's permission. Her self-esteem was non-existent – thanks to her believing his lies of how unremarkable her life was. Unfortunately, she refused to remember how prosperous her life was before she met her husband.

Thankfully, after a few years, she realized her house was not a welcomed place for her; she left it and her man. Queen B had to start all over again with no money, no self-esteem, and – due to the drama of her marriage – no job. Her family and friends walked on eggshells, afraid that constantly reminding her of their warnings to not marry her husband would cause a nervous breakdown and more depression.

Although this queen was duped into feeling undeserving, if she would have distanced herself from the negativity of her marriage and surrounded herself with those who supported and uplifted her, she would have once again believed she was capable, worthy, and significant. Her message, when she finally came to herself was, *"Get up, brush off, and get back into the game! Life goes on. I will not let it go on without me."*

4
IT TAKES TWO

Two excuses given as justification for affairs are: *"My husband or wife will not communicate with me,"* and *"My wife will not give me what I want in bed."* By no means are these the only reasons infidelity occurs. But whatever the reason, most common is the refusal of the guilty to accept the responsibility of blame for breaking their marriage covenant. According to the guilty partner, the spouse who remains faithful is the party at fault for the indiscretion.

Truthfully, it really takes two. No one else is to blame but the individuals involved in the act of adultery. Scripture says,

"But every man is tempted, when he is drawn away of his own lust, and enticed. Then when lust hath conceived, it bringeth forth sin: and sin, when it is finished, bringeth forth death." ***James 1: 14, 15***

In a compromising position, one must decide which state of mind will win, the flesh or the spirit. The Bible also says in ***James 4:7b*** to, *"Resist the devil, and he will flee from you."*

From the beginning of time, man and woman played the blame game. Adam blamed God for being tempted by the woman He gave him and Eve blamed her sin on the serpent. If the serpent had been given say in the matter, he probably would have given God an excuse, also.

There is always someone or something else to blame, but this does nothing to correct the situation. The best thing to do is own up and do right next time.

5

DEAD WOMAN WALKING

Some women across the world, are living under such strained circumstances, they have given up on hope and of a better situation. They simply exist. Their routine is to get up in the morning, prepare for the day; then, in the evening, go back to bed hoping for a good night's rest, before the alarm goes off the next day.

Many women are working jobs they do not like, to make ends meet, for bosses who do not like them or vice versa. They are living in a perpetual cycle of discontent. But they must withstand to maintain. Some other women work because they want and like to. For the vast majority who have no other choice, their work day begins at their job, continues when they get home to their families, if they have them, with cooking, cleaning, washing, ironing, homework, etc. Additionally, if she is married, the Bible explains in **I Corinthians 7:34b** that she must know, *"how she may please her husband."* So, the duties this woman fulfills do not end until her eyes are closed for the night.

If this woman has a husband who is not empathetic, sympathetic, or willing to help ease her burdens at home - especially when she is obviously overwhelmed with the strain of having to both work and take care of her family - soon she will become weary and her health may decline. Too often, many women die before their time because the physiological, psychological, and spiritual support she needed was absent. Consequently, women walk around all the time feeling obligated: obligated to their jobs, to their children, to their home, and to their husbands. Whatever is done is done because of a sense of duty.

These obligations and duties are not, by no means, trivial. The problem comes when the weight of responsibilities on the spirit becomes too much to endure. Her attempting to please everyone in her life but neglecting herself is not profitable for her or those she loves. If she is broken, tired, and deflated everyone around her suffers.

A passion to sustain happiness and to maintain a healthy body, spirit, and mind must be within her and activated without. It is not only important, but imperative, that she takes care of herself. Her life depends on it.

6

THE STRESS FACTOR

Life throws curveballs, sometimes. Some are tackled; others are met with uncertainty because of being ill prepared to deal with the challenge it presents. Then, sometimes a battle has begun before knowledge of it exists. Going from one thing to the next, one battle to the next, one trial to the next, one circumstance to the next can eventually become overwhelming.

Armor can be used to win one battle and before an exhale, another fight has come. Women can never sit back on their laurels and complain or do nothing. Women are queens and have the unique ability to wear many hats, (or crowns) if you will. So ladies should do as the old adage advises and *"choose your battles"*, carefully.

There is also an adage that states, *"Your circumstances matter less than your responses to them."* Responding to difficult circumstances can often lead to stress and many women are sick and afflicted because of the overload. Some of these hats must be shared, some placed on the shelf for a later date, and some discarded, completely. If the woman is stressed out, the whole house is stressed. Women are supposed to be builders of the house.

As far as building is concerned, the

woman who is over taxed mentally should symbolically build roadblocks and place detour signs all around for protection against psychological meltdown. Her taking time to rest in solitude without guilt and making her health and well being a priority will give her peace of mind, body, and spirit.

7

ENOUGH IS ENOUGH

On the one hand, women act like queens and, for the most part, feel like, and, upon insistence, are treated like queens – and are complete, confident, and royal (on some days). On the other hand, some days these same queens feel like slaves when fulfilling the role of: the cook, the butler, the maid, the chauffeur, the employee, the entrepreneur, and, then, late at night, the reciprocating partner and lover. They have to say yes to it all or else they have failed to perform their duty.

At the same time, some women have both the status of queens and the position of servitude. They feel the presence of happiness, success, productivity, and the pressure of failure when a task is left undone. They feel both the peace that comes with godly relationships and the evil from unhealthy attachments. When women understand and remember the two roles queens play, they should not grow discouraged when faced with these contrasting duties.

Queens depend upon their innate power and strength to overcome. They prevail against feelings of inadequacy, incompetence, and alienation. Queens persevere through obstacles and challenges. They understand that troubles only last for a little while.

The queen should be able to rest in

what her husband or companion can or is willing to do, if she has one. Also, whether married or single, she should patiently wait for God to guide and direct her towards His will. There must be a balance in her life. She cannot allow herself to be pressured into believing nothing can be assigned to a later time or a decision has to be made before all the alternatives and facts are discovered. The key is for her to keep her home, personal, professional, and spiritual life intact.

Before the queen gets to the breaking point, she should know when it is time to say, "Enough is enough."

8
C THE QUEEN

QUEEN C believes she has it all. Although, she was not born into a privileged family or the beneficiary of a large inheritance, she has done well for herself, financially. She is educated and has a prestigious career within the industry she loves. She finds fulfillment in the demands of her job, wears a mantra of arrogance, is a meticulous perfectionist, and is often dubbed as an unscrupulous go-getter. She has even been described, by most, as shallow and fake. So, what is her story?

~QUEEN C~

Most anyone who would dare stay, for any length of time, around Queen C could see through the façade she portrayed. She could too, if she had taken the time to self-reflect, which she, of course, never did. Only the few she could tolerate were allowed in her inner sanctum. Unfortunately, she was an intelligent, successful businesswoman who isolated others with her superiority complex.

Her problem? She sabotaged interpersonal relationships. As a result, her personal life suffered. If a man was interested in her, the courtship usually ended abruptly and the men failed to enlighten her of their distaste for her superficial attitude. She believed the issue lied with them not being able to handle a strong-willed woman like her...if she only knew the truth.

In her mind, she was the only queen. No other woman was a better wife, church member, or committee leader. She convinced those unfamiliar with her that she was their best choice for getting things done. But in actuality, she attempted to be involved with everything for fear of being ostracized. So she commandeered spaces and conversations to stay in the know and by the time anyone realized what she had done, she had infiltrated the scene, already.

On first glance, many women were intimidated by and envious of her, but needed not be. Queen C appeared polished and happy, however, she was depressed and lonely – not wanting to accept the emptiness her choices had created. She masked her true emotions and lied to maintain her façade in public.

But, when no one could see or hear her, the tears fell and her heartbreak continued. The cycle that started anew in the morning is embodied in the quote,

"We are so accustomed to disguise ourselves to others, that in the end, we become disguised to ourselves." -Francois de le Rochefoucauld

The sad thought is, she was concerned more for what people thought of her but they had little or no care for her. Their concern was *"my four and no more."* A real friend would have accepted her with no put ons, no snake oil, no masks, no lies; but she has no friends - none.

9

THE ORIGINAL INTENT
(THANK YOU, JANICE)

Often times, children of God make certain plans for their lives and work hard to ensure those plans are fulfilled. However, if God is not consulted first, He can delay manifesting His promises to those who refuse to inquire with Him first about their endeavors. God declares in **Jeremiah 29:11,** *"For I know the thoughts/plans that I think toward you... ...thoughts of peace, and not of evil, to give you an expected end."*

Strategic timing is also involved in the fulfillment of God's promises. Believing God fulfills His word and promises, both in relation to the fullness of His redemptive purpose and in response to the earnest prayers of His faithful people, is essential.

If believers have faith that God hears them when they petition Him for guidance to His will for their lives, they should also believe He will answer them when they seek Him. Every effort must be made to offer prayer that is parallel to His plans.

If any pulling or tugging exists in believers' spirits, it comes from their disunion from God, which causes misdirection in their lives. But, when they get with God's plans for their lives, the journey gets easier, the load gets lighter, and the vision gets clearer.

God knows the journeys we all will

take and how long the trip will last before it is complete. Berating ourselves for the diversions and recalculations that occurred along the way is useless and devoid of purpose. Thank God for His longsuffering, mercy, and grace toward us.

The timing of God's answers to prayers is often linked to God's purpose for us. The times our relationship with God goes lacking increases the delay of what God has planned for us.

When we get in the habit of being in God's will, the comfort, peace, and joy may seem unexplainable. Yet, the answer is very simple. We are in the will of God.

God is present during the trials and the tribulations of His people, and in those times, The Bible declares, *"we glory in tribulation…"* Troubles and afflictions, and even sicknesses are not meant to last. It is God's Original Intent for believers to go through these issues, not set up house with them. If our lives are to be an example and *"prosper and be in health even as their relationship with God prospers,"* God's help is the key to attaining what the Word of God says.

In between the doubt, depression, discouragement, and feeling helpless, is time. This time could be spent in prayer, seeking God's will, or becoming inundated in self-pity and hopelessness. In the meantime, the clock ticks, the calendar is flipped, and time is wasting.

10
HIGH HEEL SHOES

When women wear certain high heel shoes, the ones three inches or more, a particular attitude dominates. Call it, the sexy. Certain heels make women feel more feminine and draw attention toward them. When women feel sexy, not only will they have the demeanor to match it, they will have the walk, also. The walking becomes more intentional, especially, if a male is watching.

Depending on the outfit or footwear, a spirit can present itself attempting to align with that person's natural desires which could culminate in that individual fulfilling a fleshly purpose. Therefore, it is imperative for a godly woman to examine herself and the intent of her outfit choice, shoes included, to be sure the look and intent will honor her and God.

A sexy, sensual, provocative look should not be described of a child of God. In the New Testament, Paul always admonished the saints to live godly and in **I Thessalonians 4:4**, he exhorts the saints to present themselves as sanctified and honorable before men and God.

If sexy is all that impresses a man about a woman, then sexy will be the reason he is attracted to another, also. A woman should always look, smell, and be good, as well as seek ways to enhance her natural appearance, but it is very important her motives are pure.

There are some women who do not have to put forth any effort to be or look sexy, but, if a queen focuses on her appearance to the point of excess, to gain the attention of a man, her natural attraction can be compromised. A fine line exists between sexy and beautiful.

One can be beautiful without looking sexy, and it may be possible to be sexy without beauty. The flesh is a strange thing. Some may smile at what many call sexy; others may laugh or be repulsed. Not only is beauty in the eye of the beholder, but so is sexy.

It is not always the clothes, but it is the spirit in which they are worn that can distinguish a woman from looking beautiful and honoring God in her attire to her considered worldly in appearance and, inciting a carnal response from a male. Whatever the woman wears, her desire should be to reflect the glory given to her by God, intrinsically and from birth. Honor lasts, but sexy is not always guaranteed.

11
...AND THE KING?

Throughout history, there are many stories, but the man, for one reason or another, is not mentioned. However, the onus, this time, will be squarely on the man, the king. Most often, he is given the instructions for the family. He is the *"head"* of the woman, the queen.

"Likewise, ye husbands, dwell with them according to knowledge, giving honor unto the wife...that your prayers be not hindered."
I Peter 3:7

"So ought men to love their wives as their own bodies. He that loves his wife loves himself." **Ephesians 5:28**

"Husbands love your wives and be not bitter against them." **Colossians 3:19**

"Love your wives, even as Christ also loved the church, and gave Himself for it." **Ephesians 5:25**

The operative words of those scriptures are love and honor. Yet, other descriptive words and phrases are relevant to the attitude and responsibility a husband should have towards his wife. Words such as *"rejoice," "good thing,"* and *"joyfully,"* which relegates duties the king should not take lightly.

In the beginning of Genesis, when Eve was conversing with the serpent, scripture does not address Adam's exact location in the garden. However, he had to have been close because it reads *"she gave also unto her husband with her."* The outcome could have been different for Adam, if he had obeyed the instructions given to him by God. But many different outcomes could have birthed out of the Garden of Eden and the first couple's story.

If a king really knows his queen (her weaknesses and strengths) then keeping her in sight, both physically and spiritually, is vital. For example, if Lot was closer to his wife (in **Genesis chapter 19**) or had kept his eyes on her, at least until they reached their destination, (knowing she had issues leaving their home and possessions behind) maybe he could have kept her from looking back or being turned into a pillar of salt.

Queen Vashti may have responded differently to King Xerxes (in the book of Esther), if he had decided not to be persuaded by the demands of his male guests, alcohol, and pride. The New Testament offers examples of females without a king in their lives - the Adulterous Woman and the Woman at the Well.

As *"the head"*, the king's duty is to protect, cover, and keep the queen, in plain view - as much as possible. If he does his part, she will thank him for providing and taking care of her. But the queen still needs understanding, *"as unto the weaker vessel."*

The queen wants and expects the king to be concerned if she is treated unjustly and improperly. This means her king is around to see and hear what is occurring in his queen's life.

Everyone pays the price for the choices they make, in one way or another; as the queens aforementioned did. But, their struggles and decisions could have been different if the kings, their kings, were more attentive to their queens. The kings could have been more hands on, attentive, and concerned.

In some households, queens have to make serious decisions without the support of their king. He may not be around or if he is, other things or people occupy his time and attention. Then, other women may come from a different perspective. Their kings are around so much that getting rid of them is virtually impossible. So they use the following quote to forewarn other queens of choosing the wrong man to marry, *"Be careful what you wish for because you just might get it."*

12
FIT FOR A QUEEN

When everything is said and done, in the end, there are more than the three descriptions of women submitted in this writing that could have been discussed. For, queens come in all colors, shapes, sizes, attitudes, characteristics, and personalities. What is different, in all of them, is their personal relationship with God. This differs throughout the globe. Yet God requires the same from everyone.

In other words, God intends for a woman (if there is a man in her life) to see that man through His eyes. Not as he is. Not as he treats her. Not as he communicates with her: but as the man whom God intends for him to be. That man may not be visible yet. But, she must believe God to manifest His plan through that man in her life.

The queen is not expected to give over her entire being to the king of her life, but he is to lead her. Some men have disqualified themselves. Some are idiots. Women living in those circumstances should not be under any obligation to follow an idiot or one who has no desire to be the leader.

The queen submits to the king's lead. The king, on the other hand, submits to the queen's needs. God is the God of order. The order in the home is simple.

The head, of every woman, is the man. The head, of every man, is Jesus, and the head, of Jesus, is God.

Every man is different and many do not require or expect servitude from his woman. But, some men do, unfortunately.

In some instances, if the man does not accept his God-given responsibilities, the queen must have wisdom. For scripture says in **Proverbs 14:1**, *"The wise woman builds her house, but a foolish woman tears it down with her own hands."* If she is married to a man who is unwilling to participate in the success of their marriage, she must pray for the wisdom of God to live in that environment. That does not mean she should live in a harmful or life-threatening situation, though.

The woman is the helpmate for the man. She seeks to do those things that are pleasing to her mate. She respects him and accepts his leadership. When called on for input or suggestions, she should always be prepared and have productive input. She does not have to be right all of the time; however, she should feel her husband values her opinions and welcomes her contributions.

There is always the right time and place for conversation. Often times, the woman will choose the wrong time, the wrong place, the wrong atmosphere, the wrong everything to talk. Before speaking to her husband about a concern, sometimes, it is necessary to take a breath—a deep one—and think for a minute on whether the setting is appropriate. A woman should practice using restraint with her words and to choose her battles.

If a woman is married to a man who does not believe in her or one who is adulterous, much prayer is needed for those relationships. Maybe someday these men will learn God gave those wives for more than their physical needs. Until such time, **Jude 1:24-25** is encouragement for these women, and it reads, *"Now unto him that is able to keep you from falling, and to present you faultless before the presence of his glory with exceeding joy, To the only wise God our Saviour, be glory and majesty, dominion and power, both now and ever. Amen."*

In God there is no failure. *"When all has been done to stand...stand."* **Ephesians 6:13c**

ABOUT THE AUTHOR

The sixth of seven children, by wonderful parents, Valerie was born in Beaufort and raised on St. Helena Island in South Carolina. Although Holiness was all she knew from childhood, Valerie did not give her life completely to God until she was invited, as a sophomore attending Hampton Institute, to St. John Church of God in Christ (COGIC), in Newport News, VA. Valerie met her husband, Calvin, in church over 30 years ago. From attending church and listening to her spiritual leaders, she learned how to be a "good thing", live holy, love her neighbor, and is daily learning how to endure hardship as a good soldier of the cross. Today, Valerie realizes that whatever she is going through, whatever the trial, or test, God's Word promises, "to do exceeding abundantly above all that we ask or think, according to the power that worketh in us."

www.ingramcontent.com/pod-product-compliance
Lightning Source LLC
Chambersburg PA
CBHW071429040426
42445CB00012BA/1319